Rideshare Driver Tax Guide

Maximize Your Earnings as an Uber or Lyft Driver

Joseph Starzyk

Copyright © 2019 Joseph Starzyk

All rights reserved. No part of this publication may be reproduced, distributed or transmitted in any form or by any means, without prior written permission.

This publication is intended to provide accurate and authoritative information with regard to the subject matter covered. It is offered with the understanding that neither the publisher nor the author is engaged in rendering legal, tax or other professional services. If legal, tax or other expert assistance is required, the services of a professional should be sought.

ISBN: 1542773482
ISBN-13: 978-1542773485

Table of Contents

Chapter 1: Income Taxes 1

Chapter 2: Self-Employment Income and the Dreaded Self-Employment Tax 3

Chapter 3: Form 1099-MISC and Form 1099-K 7

Chapter 4: Quarterly Estimates 9

Chapter 5: Standard Mileage Rate vs. Actual Expense Method 15

Chapter 6: Tracking Business Mileage 19

Chapter 7: Maintaining a Proper Mileage Log 23

Chapter 8: Deductible Business Expenses 27

Chapter 9: Deducting a Business Loss 33

Chapter 10: Documentation and Recordkeeping Requirements 37

Chapter 11: The Forms and Schedules Required to Prepare Your Tax Return 39

Chapter 12: How to Prepare Your Tax Return 45

Chapter 13: Other Rideshare Tax Items 51

Chapter 1:
Income Taxes

Taxes. You can't live with them, but, unfortunately, it's hard to live without them. If you are a rideshare (Uber or Lyft) driver, you will soon discover the additional complexities that arise – that is, if you have not already. Hopefully this book will help simplify the process for you, while also providing you with the tools and information needed to successfully minimize your tax burden and prepare your own tax return.

Before we get too far into the minutiae, an overview of the U.S. federal income tax system is required. The amount of tax you owe, any eligible tax credits, and the amount of tax already paid to the government, determines whether or not you are entitled to a refund or if you owe money. Not too bad right? Well... theoretically it doesn't seem bad, but once you get into the specific rules of income, subtractions, and tax credits, things can get very complicated very quickly. Rest assured, most people do in fact feel comfortable preparing their own returns. It all depends on the level of complexity and your willingness to learn. If your goal is to be able to comfortably prepare your income tax return, this book will help get you there.

When it comes to taxes, everything starts with income. Whether the money comes from your job, your driving, maybe you own some shares that pay dividends, or maybe you even won the lottery (lucky you), these are all taxable sources of income. The goal of Form 1040, or 1040A/1040EZ depending on the level of complexity, is to take all of that income and subtract out your adjustments to arrive at your adjusted gross income. From your adjusted gross income, or AGI, you would subtract a deduction for your exemptions and your standard or itemized deductions to arrive at what is referred to as taxable income. From this taxable income, you are charged a specific amount of tax depending on your situation. Items that affect this include your filing status (single, married, head of household, etc.) and the level of your income (your tax bracket).

We now know how much income tax you owe, but that is not the end of it. There are other factors that play into the end amount of taxes owed – self-employment tax being one of them. As a ride share driver, you are effectively your own boss, as such self-employment taxes are an important factor to consider. In the next chapter, we will look in detail at self-employment tax and how this can affect your liability.

Chapter 2: Self-Employment Income and the Dreaded Self-Employment Tax

If you are a driver for Uber or Lyft, you are considered an independent contractor and chances are you will be paying self-employment tax. Self-employment tax is calculated on the net income from your business. If you're thinking to yourself that you don't have a business, well, think again. For tax purposes, working as an independent contractor means you are running your own business. Said differently, this means you are self-employed for tax purposes.

Self-employment tax is another way of describing payroll taxes. Payroll taxes include Social Security and Medicare taxes. Most people never have to deal with self-employment tax because they are only working as employees for other companies, and not for themselves. As an employee, your payroll taxes are automatically withheld from your paycheck and there is nothing further that you need to do. On the employer's side, they are also paying these same payroll taxes and will deduct them as a business expense. Together with your withholdings, they would remit this full amount to the government.

Self-employment tax is the combination of an employee's and employer's share of payroll taxes. As a contractor, no one is withholding payroll taxes for you, as you are self-employed. Thus, you would owe the combination of the two (employee and employer portions) calculated based on your business income, generally using a rate of 15.3%. You may be required to pay quarterly estimates on the amount of tax you expect to owe. We will cover quarterly estimates in more detail in Chapter 4.

As a rideshare driver, you will receive a Form 1099-K, and maybe a Form 1099-MISC, as opposed to the W-2 that you would get from an employer. I will provide more details on these forms in the next chapter. Self-employment tax is not as evil as people often make it out to be. You are entitled to certain deductions to reduce your self-employment income. You also get to deduct half of the self-employment tax owed. This is done to try to equalize the self-employed with the employer and employee relationship.

The shock surrounding self-employment taxes often comes from the high tax bill a taxpayer might not find out about until filing their tax return. Since these taxes are not being paid throughout the year through your paycheck, the tax bill can grow quite large very quickly.

A benefit of self-employment tax that is often forgot about: your payments will go to your social security fund to help fund your retirement, just as it would if you were an employee of a company. While retirement planning is beyond the scope of this book, it is good to keep in mind that there is a possibility that a chunk of the self-employment tax you pay may come back to you one day.

Chapter 3: Form 1099-MISC and Form 1099-K

There are the two main tax forms you will encounter as a rideshare driver: the Form 1099-MISC and the relatively new Form 1099-K. Uber and Lyft have started using the Form 1099-K along with the Form 1099-MISC to report taxable income. These forms report payments made to individuals for the year. Many people may be familiar with the Form 1099-MISC that companies use to report payments to independent contractors. But a Form 1099-K could be completely foreign to them.

The good news is that the Form 1099-K is substantially similar to a Form 1099-MISC. They are both going to report the total income you earned during the year. Both are designed to increase tax compliance. The IRS will be looking to tie the income shown on the form(s) with what you reported on Schedule C.

The Form 1099-K deals with third party payments, such as credit card transactions. Since Uber and Lyft process payment transactions on your behalf, they have determined that the income you earn from driving is most appropriately reported on Form 1099-K. Truth be told, it really does not make a difference to you which form you receive. You would end up reporting the same amount of income either way.

Form 1099-MISC is being used by Uber and Lyft to report incentive payments or other bonuses you may have received. Essentially, any payment that these companies made directly to you will be reported on Form 1099-MISC. This is as opposed to Uber and Lyft first collecting a fee from the passenger, and then remitting a portion of that fee to you. The income is reported the same way as from a Form 1099-K and will flow to Schedule C either way.

The amount shown on the forms may actually be higher than the payments you received. Generally, this is not a mistake. The difference between what you received and the amount reported on the Form 1099-K or Form 1099-MISC are fees paid to the company. As we will see later, you can deduct these fees, along with any other applicable deductions.

Keep in mind, you may have received other payments that were not reported to you. For example, if you are an Uber driver and someone leaves you a cash tip. The tip is reportable income and should be included in the total gross income you report for the year.

Chapter 4:
Quarterly Estimates

Quarterly estimate payments are used to pay some, or all, of your taxes owed before the actual filing of your tax return. In certain situations, they are required. If they were required, and you did not pay any or did not pay enough, you could be subject to an underpayment penalty when you file your tax return. The amount of the penalty varies considerably depending on your situation. It could be anywhere from a few dollars to several hundred dollars. For this reason, it is important to understand what the minimum amount you need to pay in is for any given year. I will explain how you can avoid the underpayment penalty even if you do not pay in 90% of your current year taxes due.

In most cases, you must pay quarterly estimated taxes for the current year if both of the following apply:

1. You expect to owe at least $1,000 in tax for the year, after subtracting your withholdings and any credits you may be getting; and

2. Your total withholdings and credits are less than the smaller of: 90% of the taxes owed on your current return, or 100% (in some cases 110%) of the taxes shown on your prior year tax return.

Both of these scenarios are worth further discussion. In scenario one above, if you are a full-time rideshare driver, there is actually a chance that you will owe less than $1,000 worth of tax for the year. How profitable your driving is largely depends on your local market. If you end up driving many dead miles, which we will go over later, your mileage deduction could wipe out the majority of your income. For a single filer, you would need just over $7,000 of profit (not gross receipts) to reach that $1,000 threshold assuming no other sources of income. While achievable for many, it is not unusual for your net profit to be lower than that.

To summarize, if you are a full-time single rideshare driver with no other sources of income, you do not need to make quarterly estimates to avoid the underpayment penalty so long as you expect your net profit to be $7,000 or less. If you think your net profit will be over $7,000, then you should plan to make estimated payments to avoid penalties. The last couple paragraphs of this chapter detail out how to make these payments.

The first part of scenario two informs us that we need to cover at least 90% of the current year tax owed to avoid an underpayment penalty. This would involve estimating your income and estimated tax liability on a quarterly basis. With that, you would determine how much tax would be owed and would pay the appropriate estimate. It is often very cumbersome and should only be used when required. If you did not file a tax return in the prior year, or if you did not owe any tax on the prior year return, then you must follow this guideline.

The second part of scenario two above (100% or 110% of the taxes shown on your prior year tax return) is what tax practitioners typically rely on when providing estimates to their clients. And this is done for good reason. It is my recommended option when you are expecting either similar or greater income than the previous year. Most individuals will fall into this category for determining estimates.

The IRS is basically saying that you can ignore everything going on in the current year and instead base your quarterly estimates on the tax you owed in the prior year. If your adjusted gross income is $150,000 or less, you are required to pay in 100% of your prior year tax. Your prior year total tax can be found on the last line in the "Other Taxes" section on page 2 of Form 1040. Currently, this is Line 63, but it can change year to year. If your adjusted gross income is above $150,000, then you are required to pay in 110% of your prior year tax. In either case, you are required to pay $1/4^{th}$ of your required tax each quarter.

If you follow this recommendation, keep in mind you still may owe a hefty sum when you file your tax return. You will not, however, owe any underpayment penalties. It is a good idea to at least have a ballpark estimate of your income and estimated tax liability for the year so you can set aside some cash to cover your tax liability.

For those that have a full-time job and are doing rideshare driving on the side, you have another option available to you. If you are an employee, you typically do not have to worry about quarterly estimates because your employer withholds your federal taxes automatically. You can actually use this to your advantage. You can change the amount that they withhold to adjust to your individual needs.

For example, let's say you are having $100 withheld each week towards your federal withholding at your full-time job. That equates to $5,200 for the year. If your adjusted gross income in the prior year was under $150,000, you would look to see if the $5,200 is at least equal to your prior year tax. If the answer is yes, then you are all set. You do not need to worry about estimates or changing your withholding. If, however, you see that you owed $6,000 in tax in the prior year, you need to update your withholdings if you are expecting similar or greater income this year. You would submit an updated Form W-4 to your employer to instruct them how much additional tax you want withheld (Line 6 of the form). Let us say you noticed this sometime in May, so there are about 32 weeks left in the year. You would need an additional $25 of withholding per paycheck to meet your required $6,000 in withholding for the year.

For those that would need to make quarterly estimates and wish to pay the old-fashioned way via a paper voucher, the current quarterly estimated tax vouchers can be found at the following link:

https://www.irs.gov/pub/irs-pdf/f1040es.pdf

Conveniently, the IRS also lets you make quarterly estimated payments online. The link to make those payments is:

https://www.irs.gov/payments/direct-pay

Quarterly estimated payments are due by April 15th, June 15th, September 15th, and January 15th. If any of those days fall on a federal holiday or a weekend, then the deadline is the next business day.

Chapter 5: Standard Mileage Rate vs. Actual Expense Method

Rideshare drivers actually have two options for deducting auto expenses attributed to driving passengers for hire. These methods include the standard mileage rate method and the actual expense method. Your total deduction and recordkeeping requirements differ depending on which method you choose. There are certain opportunities that will allow you to switch between methods each year. This way, you can pick the most beneficial method for any given year. More details on this at the end of the chapter.

The standard mileage rate gives you a deduction equal to the total business miles you drove for the year times the standard mileage rate. In 2018, the standard mileage rate was 54.5 cents per mile. In 2019, it is 58 cents per mile. We will use the 2018 rates to illustrate. For example, if your total miles for the year were 10,000, and 4,000 of those were business miles, your deduction would be $2,180 (4,000 * $0.535 = $2,180). Aside from some information about your vehicle, the business mileage driven via a mileage log, and some form of corroborating evidence (such as your Uber or Lyft statements), you do not need any other support for this deduction. The key is to maintain a proper mileage log to ensure you maximize your deduction. More details on deductible miles and your mileage log in the next two chapters. You can visit http://www.irs.gov/Tax-Professionals/Standard-Mileage-Rates to obtain the current year's mileage rate.

The actual expense method allows you to deduct the business portion of auto related expenses that you incurred during the year, based on the percent of business mileage driven to total miles for the year. Some of these expenses include: gas, oil, tires, lease payments, maintenance, repairs, insurance, registration fees, and depreciation. For example, let's say you spent about $1,200 on gas, $1,000 on insurance, $500 for new tires and $300 for some oil changes (ignoring depreciation). This comes out to $3,000 of actual expenses incurred for the year. You would then take this amount and multiply it by the ratio of your business to total use of your vehicle. Following our previous example, this would be $3,000 * (4,000/10,000) = $1,200. For this method, you would need to keep your receipts/documentation for all applicable expenses in addition to your mileage log. You are not allowed to deduct any mileage.

Using our hypothetical numbers, the standard mileage rate method is more beneficial for you to use in the current year. Keep in mind that this could change each year.

While it requires more work and more recordkeeping, though rare, you may end up with a larger deduction by using the actual expense method. One of the largest tax benefits is being able to take a depreciation deduction for your vehicle. This means you would be able to deduct a certain percentage of the price that you paid for your vehicle each year. Assuming you use your car 50% or less (determined by your mileage driven) for your rideshare business, you would be able to deduct the cost of your car equally over 5 years. The amount deducted is based on your business use, and it is also subject to annual limits set by the IRS for passenger autos. For cars placed in service in 2018, this limit is $10,000 for both passenger autos and light duty trucks/vans (a significant increase from 2017 limits). The vehicle may also qualify for an additional $8,000 first-year bonus depreciation deduction.

If you are not sure which method may be right for you, I would recommend tracking both for your first year of driving. It is a bit tedious, but it can be hard to guess which method is best. Many find that the standard mileage rate method is not only easier to keep track of, but typically results in a higher deduction too. If you do not feel like taking the time to use the actual expense method, rest assured that the standard mileage rate method is probably your best choice anyways.

Certain limitations apply for switching back and forth between the actual expense method and the standard mileage rate. If you want to use the standard mileage rate, you must choose that in the first year your car is used for business purposes. Then, in later years, you can choose either method provided you meet the following criteria: you own the car (not a lease) and you use the straight-line method of depreciation when using actual expenses. This means no MACRS depreciation, bonus depreciation or a Section 179 deduction for your vehicle.

There are certain auto related expenses that you get to deduct regardless of which method you choose. Examples of these include: parking fees, tolls, auto loan interest and personal property taxes. Again, you would need to keep accurate records of these expenses. A detailed discussion of possible business expenses that apply regardless of which auto expense method you choose follows later in the book.

Chapter 6: Tracking Business Mileage

Now you know that tracking your business mileage is important for both the standard mileage rate method and the actual expense method. The next question would be, what exactly are deductible business miles for a rideshare driver? There are certain situations where the miles driven are certainly deductible, but other situations are not as clear-cut. This chapter will go through the most common scenarios to get you started in the right direction.

First, let us get the obvious one out of the way. If you are doing some rideshare driving, the mileage you incur while transporting passengers in your car is deductible. No questions asked here. Just make sure to keep an accurate mileage log, which we will discuss in the next chapter, and this one is done.

Next, we have the mileage going from one passenger pick-up to the next. For example, it's a busy night. You drop the passenger off at their destination, and you immediately get a ping for another pick-up. You proceed the 4 miles to get to the new passenger's pick-up location. Though some may disagree, I believe this mileage to be deductible. There is no doubt you are on the job, and you are driving to the next passenger to continue earning money for the night. This is deductible business mileage. Again, be sure to keep a log of this.

Following the same logic as the previous example, you may have mileage incurred driving to a destination area. If you are driving to get to a better location for passenger pick-ups (or for a surge), deduct that mileage as well.

Then, we have a bit of a gray area regarding the initial pick-up and final passenger drop-off for the night. Some people do not have the luxury of sitting at home waiting for a ping to head out a few blocks to start working. Instead, they might make a trip of 10-15 miles into the city to be in a better location. If your intent is to drive into the city to be in a better location to work for the night, this mileage is deductible. You can also include your return trip back home. Basically, as soon as you leave your house to make some money you are considered working, and those miles should be deducted.

Intent is the key in the previous example. You cannot just load your app and drive into the city to go to the mall and expect those miles to be deductible. You were never intending to solely work in the first place, and thus, those miles would be considered personal. Intent can be difficult to prove either way. It is helpful to have some completed trips at the destination area to prove the business purpose of the trip.

If you are driving out to get some gas prior to a night of rideshare driving, those miles are deductible. If you make a quick detour to get some gas while out driving for the night, this follows the same logic – those miles are deductible. If you need to make a supply run, deduct the miles you drove for that. By supplies, this would include items for you, your car, or your passengers for rideshare driving. Note in your mileage log the reason for the trip and the expenses incurred.

It is impossible to go through every scenario, but the items presented here should give you a great start. The key take-away is understanding that intent is the most important aspect. If you are intending to work, to drive and pick up passengers, or make deliveries and earn some income, then those miles are deductible.

Chapter 7: Maintaining a Proper Mileage Log

A mileage log is probably the single most important item of tax support for a rideshare driver. Your auto deduction is going to be your highest expense, and a mileage log is what is used to track and substantiate that deduction.

Nowadays, there are three different ways of tracking and maintaining your mileage log. As long as all the needed information is recorded and kept in your records, you can choose to use any combination of the three methods.

You need to track the following information:

- Date
- Destination/Area
- Business purpose (e.g. Uber driving, getting gas, etc.)
- Beginning and ending odometer readings for the year
- Miles for the trip (ideally with starting and ending odometer readings, but not required)

- Description and amount for any relevant expenses for the trip

It seems like a lot to track, but it's really not so bad once you get used it. The IRS does require a contemporaneous mileage log. This means, you should be keeping track of your business mileage as you go, day by day. You cannot, and should not, recreate your mileage log after-the-fact.

The first method to track your mileage is via an old-fashioned day planner or journal. Keep the journal in your car. Note your starting odometer reading on January 1 (or the day you start your rideshare business) of the year and your ending odometer reading on December 31st of the year. Then, every time you go into your car to do some rideshare driving, note your starting odometer. Once you finish driving for the night, note your ending odometer reading. And that's it. You now have your business miles recorded for each rideshare driving session. No notations are required for your personal driving unless they coincide with a business trip.

You would calculate your total mileage for the year by using your starting and ending odometer readings on January 1 and December 31. You need to add up all of your business trips. Then, whatever the difference is would be considered personal non-deductible mileage and this is also reported on your tax return.

The second method follows all of the same requirements as the first. Instead of, or in addition to, the day planner or journal, you would input all the same data into an excel sheet. This will make calculations easier. An excel sheet can also be backed up, saved to the cloud, or however you want to store it for easy retrieval down the road if ever needed. Most drivers end up using a combination of these first two methods.

The final, and relatively new, method for tracking your business mileage is to use an app on your phone. As of this writing, there are countless apps out there that accomplish this task. Some of these include, in no particular order: Everlance, Expensify, TripLog, SherpaShare, Hurdlr for Drivers, Ride Companion, and Driver Companion. Most of these apps are available for both iOS and Android.

The apps follow the same concept as a day journal. You load the app, indicate in some fashion that you are working, and the app does the rest. It records the date & time, mileage driven, and possibly other information. I have found most to be pretty accurate. In addition, drivers who use an app are more likely to document all (or most) of their business mileage to maximize their deduction.

The important item to note surrounding apps is maintaining proper support. At the end of the year, and ideally throughout the year as well, you should export the information captured by the app to your computer. Save this document and keep it with your tax records. Unfortunately, not all apps last forever. This way, you still have support to back-up your deduction even if the app ceases to exist. Depending on the app, you may have to pay to get this information exported. Unless you want to transfer everything manually, it's worth your money.

Chapter 8:
Deductible Business Expenses

There are certain business expenses that are deductible regardless of whether you use the standard mileage rate or the actual expense method. You will want to track and deduct these expenses if they apply to you.

The first big one that applies to all drivers is your cell phone expense. If you are renting a phone or have a completely separate phone for business purposes, then you could deduct 100% of these costs. Most drivers, however, use their personal cell phone – and this is where it gets a little more complicated.

The good news is that at least a portion of your cell phone expenses is deductible. An additional plus, is that the tax court has ruled that cell phone expenditures do not fall under the broad category of "utilities." Thus, it is not necessary to maintain a home office, or any office for that matter, to deduct a reasonable portion of your cell phone bill.

Aside from using a "reasonable" method, there is no clear guidance on how to properly allocate your cell phone expenses between business and personal use. However, this step is required in order to determine the deductible amount of your personal cell phone bills. Here are a couple of options to consider:

1. Look at how much data your business apps are using vs. the rest of your phone. For example, if you use the Uber app and Google Maps for rideshare driving, and together those eat up about 2 gigs of data for your 4-gig data plan – then you could deduct approximately 50% of your cell phone expenses.

2. Try and record how much time you spend on your phone during a typical day for business and for personal use. Track the data for about a week and you should have a pretty good sample size. For example, on the first day you track your time you use your phone about 1 hour a day for personal reasons, and about 3 hours a day doing business. You find this to be consistent throughout the week. Thus, you determine that 75% of your cell phone expenses (or 3/4ths of your time) are deductible for business purposes.

These are just a couple of the more popular options. There are others ways to track your phone usage. Remember the method must be "reasonable." And whatever it is you choose, it is important to note that you should be consistent with your method. Do not switch month to month to try and get the most favorable outcome. If you later determine that a different method would give you a more accurate allocation method, you can change it. Just do not do it all the time.

Following is a list of other expenses that may apply to you. Remember to keep a record (and receipts) of these expenses to deduct them on your tax return:

- Phone chargers: If you bought a phone charger to use in your car for rideshare driving, this is currently deductible.

- Phone stands/mounts/other accessories: Same as phone charger – if bought to use for rideshare driving, this is currently deductible.

- AAA or other roadside assistance membership: Purchasing a roadside assistance membership for your rideshare driving business is 100% deductible. However, if you already had a membership prior to rideshare driving, you may want to consider allocating it between personal and business usage. You could use the personal and business mileage driven for the year, for example, to allocate the expenses between the two.

- Prescription eye glasses/contacts used only for driving: If required for driving, allocate between personal and business use. The business use portion is deductible.

- Snacks/water: If you purchase snacks and/or water solely for your riders, deduct these costs in full.

- Car washes: Any additional car washes incurred because of your rideshare driving are deductible. For example, if you typically washed your car every 3 weeks, but after driving for Uber you have to wash it every week – then you would deduct 2 of every 3 car washes. Otherwise, car washes are generally included in your auto expenses (actual expense method or standard mileage method). If you do not wash your car more often due to ridesharing, do not deduct.

- Car cleaning/detailing: This follows the same logic as car washes above.

- Air/car freshener: If bought for your rideshare driving, deduct these costs in full.

- Personal property taxes: Does your city or town charge a personal property tax on your vehicle? A portion of it can be deducted as a business expense. Use the personal vs. business mileage driven to allocate this expense. The rest of the deduction would be allocated to Schedule A if you are itemizing your deductions for the year as personal property taxes.

- Loan interest: Deduct the business portion of interest paid on a loan that is secured by your vehicle.

- Parking fees: Deduct if incurred while rideshare driving. This does not include parking tickets.

- Tolls: Deduct tolls paid while rideshare driving. Also, include tolls between passenger pick-ups and drop-offs while on the job. Tolls paid prior to starting and after ending rideshare driving are usually deductible as well, so long as rideshare driving was the purpose of your trip.

- Fees/commissions: Deduct the fees and commissions that your rideshare company automatically takes out of your earnings. Your earnings will be reported to you in gross, and must be reported on your tax return in gross. Therefore, don't forget to deduct these fees/commissions.

- Siri, magazines or other in-car entertainment: Did you purchase a subscription for your riders' enjoyment? Deduct this cost.

- Tax prep fees: A portion of your tax prep fees can be allocated to Schedule C. This is true if you use a tax preparer, or if you purchase software to do your taxes on your own.

- Meals: in certain rare cases, your meals expense could be deductible. For example, if you meet with other drivers to discuss business strategies.

This list should give you a great start, but there are other potential deductions. All of the above expenses can be used regardless of whether you are using the actual expense or standard mileage method. When facing a new type of expense, you must decide if the business expense is "ordinary and necessary" for driving. If not, chances are it is not deductible.

Starting in 2018, there is a new deduction often referred to as the 20% Pass-through deduction. Rideshare drivers will be able to utilize this deduction. The deduction would be equal to 20% of your net profit from your rideshare business. If your business has a loss, there is no deduction. Rideshare driving is not considered a specified service trade or business. You do not need to incorporate or form an LLC to be eligible to receive the deduction. If you are using tax software to complete your tax return, the deduction should be computed automatically. You'll want to verify the deduction is included on Form 1040, page 2, line 9.

Chapter 9:
Deducting a Business Loss

After completing Schedule C, which will be discussed in detail later, many drivers find that they operated at a tax loss for the year. This means their deductions exceeded their income. Two important considerations come from this result.

First, this is a good time to take a step back from the details and day-to-day items of the business and think about what is going on. Most tax losses result from a generous standard mileage deduction. Meaning, you are driving a significant amount of miles. So while you are getting money from every ride, you are deteriorating your car at an accelerated rate. This is the main trade-off for rideshare driving, and for certain cars and people it is perfectly fine. For others, it is simply not worth it. Here are some other questions to consider: Are there certain driving habits you can change? Are there areas in your market you should focus your driving in? Is your market becoming oversaturated and, thus, less profitable?

Secondly, it must be determined whether or not the loss can be used to offset other forms of income.

The concern for many drivers is whether or not you can use the loss to reduce wages or other forms of taxable income. In most cases, the answer is yes. So long as you are treating your rideshare activity as a business, you should be able to deduct your business loss against other forms of income – such as typical wage income.

A common misconception is that if your business does not show a profit in at least three of five years, then the IRS will deny your business loss and instead classify it as a hobby. You do not want your business to be classified as a hobby. Generally, hobby losses are only deductible to the extent of hobby income. And even then, the deductions for your hobby could be further limited. Starting in 2018, the new tax law eliminates hobby loss deductions completely.

It is true that the IRS will look to see if your business is profiting to help determine whether or not the activity is considered a hobby. This is not the only factor. What actually happens is that the burden of proof shifts from the IRS to the taxpayer to show that the activity is a business – not a hobby. Following is a brief discussion of nine factors that you could use to help prove that you are running a business:

1. Treat your business like a business. Do this by keeping good records and looking for ways to make the business profitable, similar to other non-rideshare businesses.

2. Develop expertise in the rideshare industry. Maybe take some courses online, print/read blogs, and stay up to date on current rideshare news and trends.
3. Put some time and effort into generating income. Do not just go out once every few weeks because you felt like it. Have a plan and show some consistency. Your driving log will help to document this plan.
4. Generate a return from your assets. This factor does not apply to rideshare drivers.
5. If you successfully ran a rideshare or limo/taxi service in the past, this could help prove you are more likely to be successful in the current business. For many, this factor may not apply.
6. As mentioned previously, your history of income and loss plays a factor. If you can show previous experience in these areas, you are more likely to be proving your case.
7. Going along with factor 6, the amount of profits vs. losses you generated in those years is also considered. There is difference between $100 of profit vs. $10,000 of profit.
8. Your financial status with and without the rideshare income is also considered. The activity can still be considered a business even if it is done as a part-time business (as most are). However, there is no doubt the

activity is a business if that is your only source of income.

9. The last factor looks at how much enjoyment you get from the business. For most, driving for hire is not generally considered "fun." This would help further your case.

There are many factors that impact your ability to deduct a business loss. You should, however, deduct whatever expenses you are entitled to. The factors could be summarized by saying: treat the business like a business. If you do that, you will likely not have any issues deducting and using the loss to offset other forms of income.

Chapter 10: Documentation and Recordkeeping Requirements

The single most important item for a rideshare driver is a current and valid mileage log. Please re-read Chapter 7 if you have to. Aside from that, there are other things you need to know about keeping records for both income and expenses.

Records of income are relatively straightforward for a rideshare driver. The records must show the amounts and sources of your gross receipts. Since Uber/Lyft deposit the money directly into your bank account, and provide you with a Form 1099, that is all the support you will need: your bank statements and copies of the Form 1099s you received. You can keep electronic copies instead of hard copies. Though not necessarily required, keeping an excel summary sheet (or similar) of monies received would be an excellent additional record to maintain.

Records of expense must show the amount paid and a description that shows the amount was for a legitimate business expense. If it is a meal expense, you should note whom the meal was with and what business was discussed. Examples of appropriate records would include cancelled checks, receipts, credit card statements, and invoices. Again, you can keep electronic copies if you wish.

The minimum amount of time to maintain your records is 3 years from the date you filed your tax return. In some cases, you may have to keep your records for up to 7 years. Thus, it is recommended to keep all records for 7 years. Records of any assets used in your business (such as your car) should be kept so long as the asset is still in-use – even if it is past the 3 (or 7) year mark. Correctly tracking and maintaining your records will make your life a lot easier should you ever be subject to an audit (discussed a little more in Chapter 13).

Chapter 11: The Forms and Schedules Required to Prepare Your Tax Return

At this point in the book, we have made it through all of the background information about rideshare taxes, which expenses are deductible, and how to keep adequate records. Next, armed with that information and your Form 1099s, comes the exciting part: preparing your tax return. First, we will discuss the necessary forms and schedules. Then, I will explain how you can file your taxes for free in the following chapter.

It is important to understand the forms and schedules you will be filing. This will allow you to take your knowledge and apply it to your tax return, regardless of what software you use to prepare it. In theory, all tax preparation software should produce the same end result on your tax forms. Any decent tax preparation software will allow you to view your actual tax forms and schedules for review prior to submitting your tax return.

If you filed Form 1040A or Form 1040EZ in the past, unfortunately that will no longer be an option for you. All tax returns that are reporting rideshare income will require Form 1040. In addition, the IRS is no longer using Form 1040A or Form 1040EZ starting with tax year 2018. For reference, you can view the current Form 1040 at the following URL: https://www.irs.gov/pub/irs-pdf/f1040.pdf

Schedule 1: https://www.irs.gov/pub/irs-pdf/f1040s1.pdf Schedule 4: https://www.irs.gov/pub/irs-pdf/f1040s4.pdf and Schedule 5: https://www.irs.gov/pub/irs-pdf/f1040s5.pdf (typing the forms into a search engine should yield the same links as above).

There were numerous updates to the form from 2017 to 2018. However, there will be very few changes, if any, for future years. The following lines would be affected for an individual reporting rideshare income (please note that I am referencing the 2018 Forms in all of the following examples, the line item references may vary slightly for other years):

- Page 2, Line 6 "Total income" – The net profit from your business will flow to this line right next to "Add any amount from Schedule 1, line 22." As noted, that amount comes from Schedule 1.

- Page 2, Line 7 "Adjusted gross income" – The deduction you receive for 50% of the self-employment tax will be deducted from the total on this line. Again, as noted, that amount comes from Schedule 1.

- Page 2, Line 9 "Qualified business income deduction" – If you have a net profit from your business, this is where the 20% pass-through deduction would be reported. See discussion at the end of Chapter 8 for more information.

- Page 2, Line 14 "Other taxes. Attach Schedule 4" – This line would have your total self-employment tax owed for the year. Comes from Schedule 4.

- Page 2, Line 17 "Add any amounts from Schedule 5" – This is where the total of all of your federal quarterly tax estimates, if any, would be reported. Comes from Schedule 5.

- Schedule 1, Line 12 "Business income or (loss). Attach Schedule C or C-EZ" – This line would have your net profit from your business. Comes from Schedule C, as noted on the line.

- Schedule 1, Line 27 "Deductible part of self-employment tax. Attach Schedule SE" – The deduction you receive for 50% of the self-employment tax paid will be deducted here. Comes from Schedule SE, as noted on the line.

- Schedule 4, Line 57 "Self-employment tax. Attach Schedule SE" – This line would have your total self-employment tax owed for the year. Again, comes from Schedule SE, as noted on the line.

- Schedule 5, Line 66 "2018 estimated tax payments and amount applied from 2017 return" – This is where the total of all of your federal quarterly tax estimates, if any, would be reported.

Next, we will talk about Schedule C – "Profit or Loss from Business." For reference, you can view the current Schedule C at the following URL: https://www.irs.gov/pub/irs-pdf/f1040sc.pdf

Schedule C is where you will report all of your income and expenses. I will cover the primary aspects of the Schedule C:

- First section, Line A "Principal business or profession" – This is where you describe your business. For example, you could use "TNC driver" (transportation network company), "Uber driver" or simply just "Driver."

- First section, Line B "Enter code from instructions" – This is the six-digit business code based on the North American Industry Classification System (NAICS). There is no perfect answer for rideshare drivers. The closest code is 485300 for Taxi & limousine service.

- Part I, Line 1 "Gross receipts or sales" – This is where you report your gross receipts for the year. That means your income before any expenses. In general, it will be the total of the revenue reported on your Form 1099-Ks and Form 1099-MISCs.

- Part II has details on all of your expenses for the year. Line 9 will be where you report your auto expenses, including your deduction for mileage driven or actual expenses. If your other expenses do not fit into one of the pre-written line items, you simply list them in Part V, as other expenses, and the total will flow to Line 27a.

Schedule C-EZ can also used to report your business activity, and is far simpler in nature. You can view the current Schedule C-EZ at the following URL https://www.irs.gov/pub/irs-pdf/f1040sce.pdf. Part I is the same as the instructions for the Section 1 noted above. All receipts are reported on Part II, Line 1 and all expenses are reported on Part II, Line 2. The catch is that not everyone is eligible to file a Schedule C-EZ. And even if you are, do note that you are still required to maintain adequate records. This is where having good documentation and an excel summary sheet (or the like) would come in handy.

The requirements to use a Schedule C-EZ are listed at the top of page. Of special note for rideshare drivers, you cannot file the C-EZ if you have more than $5,000 of business expenses or ended up with a net loss from your business.

Next, we have the Schedule SE – "Self-Employment Tax." This schedule will be included with your tax return if you have a net profit from your business. The current schedule can be found here: https://www.irs.gov/pub/irs-pdf/f1040sse.pdf

Lucky for you, this schedule should be completed automatically by your tax preparation software. Starting on Line 2, the form breaks down the calculation of your self-employment tax. The total tax is reported on Line 5 and your deduction for one-half of the tax is reported on Line 6.

Chapter 12:
How to Prepare Your Tax Return

My hope is the information presented thus far will give you the confidence needed to prepare your own tax return. Not only are there countless tax professionals willing to help you, there are also countless options for preparing your own taxes. Everyone has likely heard of the big players – TurboTax and H&R Block. The year 2017, starting with 2016 tax returns, saw an exciting new provider emerge: Credit Karma. This is actually my recommended option.

I am not affiliated with Credit Karma nor did I receive any kind of remuneration for recommending their services. I am a professional tax preparer, so many may find it strange I am suggesting a legitimate do-it-yourself option in the first place.

Credit Karma is known for providing a secure, no-hassle, zero-fee approach to tracking and keeping you up-to-date about your credit report and credit scores. They moved into the tax preparation business with this same philosophy.

Most, will in fact, qualify to prepare and e-file their federal and state return for free through Credit Karma. Other software providers frequently charge for state tax returns and/or small businesses. This is not so with Credit Karma. Form 1040, Schedule C, and Schedule SE are all included for free.

To get started, visit the following website: https://www.creditkarma.com/tax. Either sign in with your existing Credit Karma account or create a new account for free. Once logged in, navigate to the "Tax" tab (if needed) and select "Prepare my taxes/Get Started."

You should first go through and fill out your basic info. This includes items such as your name, address, date of birth, and dependent information. Once that is done, you will move on to your Federal taxes.

If at any time you wish to see how the information you have entered has changed your tax forms, you can view your tax forms by clicking on the menu in the top-left corner and selecting "My tax forms."

As mentioned previously, your rideshare income and expenses will be reported on Schedule C. You can either walk through the interview process or navigate to "Looking for something else?" -> "Self-employment or side gigs" -> then click "Start" next to "Business income (Schedule C)." You can either add the info from Form 1099-K and Form 1099-MISC or proceed directly to "Business income (Schedule C) to add your totals there.

Once there, you will need to add a new business. Fill in the business name and EIN (or leave blank if you are using your SSN for Uber/Lyft) and, in most cases, you can check off the box to use your personal address as your business address.

Next, you must select the type of business. This is to figure out your NAICS code as discussed in the previous chapter. For a rideshare driver, the best selection is "Transportation and Warehousing" followed by "Taxi & limousine service."

Next, you will likely answer "No" to the Form 1099 questions and have a $0 for prior year losses. At this point, you can also switch to "View full form" (in the top-right corner) if you wish to enter your items directly on one long screen. You can always switch back to the "View step by step" if you prefer that option.

By default, the answer to whether or not you started the business in the current year is set to "no." Update this field if appropriate in your case.

Now we have come to the income section. The first line is income from Form 1099-MISCs. If you wanted, you could go back a section to add a Form 1099-MISC and link that to this business (now that it is created). But that is not necessary. You can report the total amount on all Form 1099-MISC received in the "Gross receipts or sales" field. Then report the total of all Form 1099-Ks in the "Merchant card and third party network payments" field.

Proceed to enter your relevant business expenses. Please note, "other expenses" comes at the very end. A rideshare business is not considered a "Specified service business" and does not need to be aggregated. As you proceed through the steps, you will have the option of entering vehicle expenses. You will want to select "yes" for this. After entering your miles, you will have the option of using the standard mileage rate or actual expenses. For most drivers, the standard mileage rate option will be most beneficial. You can select "use actual expenses" to see what that deduction comes to and then come back to this screen to select the standard mileage rate. This will allow you to compare the two options and determine which one provides you with the best deduction.

Please note, if you are using the standard mileage rate, unfortunately Credit Karma does not let you enter additional deductible auto expenses. This is the one fault I have found with the software for rideshare drivers. You will have to enter additional auto expenses in the other expense section. The big three expenses that you can take even if you use the standard mileage rate include: parking fees and tolls, business portion of interest paid on a loan, and business portion of personal property taxes paid. The business portion would be your total expense multiplied by the ratio of your business miles over the total miles driven.

That should cover the rideshare portion of your taxes. Of course, you have the option of entering W-

2's and any other tax information you may need. I hope that you will find the software as intuitive as I have. Remember, you can (and should) look at your tax forms anytime by clicking on the menu in the top-left corner and selecting "My tax forms" and then opening the appropriate PDF. You should make an effort to review your actual tax forms and schedules at least once prior to submitting your returns. Though the experience can be daunting at first, the more you do it the more familiar everything will become.

Credit Karma makes their money through personalized recommendations for items such as better credit cards, loans, and insurance products. You will likely find these "ads" as you use the service.

Chapter 13: Other Rideshare Tax Items

There are a few other tax items related to rideshare driving that I would like to touch on before concluding this book. These are questions and issues that I have seen over the years that may be applicable in certain situations.

In my opinion, setting up a separate business structure for rideshare driving is simply not worth the hassle. Whether it is an S-Corp, a Limited Liability Company (LLC) taxed as a sole proprietorship, or an LLC taxed as an S-Corp, the extra time and expense rarely outweighs the benefits. For certain individuals that may need (or want) the extra liability protection, it could make sense. I do, however, recommend registering for a free EIN for your sole proprietorship business; this will allow you to not use your SSN if you are not comfortable with that (in case of a security breach, for example).

If you are the unfortunate recipient of an IRS audit, you may want to seek professional help to make sure all of your information is in order before you communicate with the IRS. Many IRS audits nowadays are "desk" or "correspondence" audits. The IRS will send a request for information to support certain items on your tax return. You make copies of the items and mail or fax them back to the IRS. If you are comfortable with it, you certainly can do it yourself. Generally, you will only want to provide the requested information (in the order requested). If the IRS needs anything else, they will follow-up with another request and you can send the information in at that point in time. The IRS is VERY slow at corresponding back and forth. The audit process is likely to draw on for quite some time depending on how backed up the IRS is.

There are resources available online if you were to search for answers to your tax questions. Unless you are using the IRS website, you should check more than one source to make sure you are getting the correct information. Remember, anyone can put information on the internet. It is often not the best source for tax information.

Though I hope this book has made you feel more prepared to do your own taxes, the option of seeking out a professional tax preparer is always available. Tax law can be pretty confusing at times, so don't feel defeated. You should seek out someone familiar with rideshare tax laws as there are certain facets that are unique to the industry. Please keep in mind this book focuses exclusively on Federal income tax issues.

Made in the USA
Middletown, DE
16 November 2019